Reflections

Thought-Provoking Antidotes for True and Lasting Change

Michael Maitre

This book is dedicated to my beloved son, Kai. You inspire me to reach, you inspire me to climb, and you inspire me to flex every muscle of my soul.

Table of Contents

~ Preface ~

Preface

The inspiration for this book came when I was in Jamaica celebrating my 4-year anniversary. I was just parting ways with 15-plus years of climbing the corporate ladder. I was at the beginning stages of starting my own wellness business from the ground up. This vacation was an important time for me to take a step back and truly make some inspired decisions about the new waters I was about to navigate. The experience out in Jamaica was nothing short of amazing. The atmosphere brought nostalgia of visiting Haiti as a child with my parents. It had the makings of a true-to-life paradise, both on and off the resort. It turned out my wife had some friends she had known since high school who coincidentally happened to be vacationing in Jamaica on the same days as we were.

One of them in particular was of Jamaican descent. This gave us the opportunities to hang out with some locals (her family) during our trip. Growing up visiting Haiti and other Caribbean islands, I knew what to expect; small, modest houses with lots of character, and roofs made of tin. Upon visiting the local neighborhoods of Montego Bay, we were immediately taken aback by many of the houses. Some of these homes stood as tall as three stories high! The sizes were comparable to what would be considered mansions in the United States. The caveat, however, was that none of these homes were completed. In fact, most if not all were abandoned. It was then that the symbolic message of this experience stood up and slapped me in the face.

There is a potential in these communities for people to reach the highest of goals and aspirations. There is truly no structure too high and no dream too impossible. The notion that these homes had potential is an understatement; but potential without a meaningful strategy is just an empty house with no roof. There is no value, no purpose; and whatever debris the winds blow in will eventually lead to its decay. The lack of a strategic plan as it relates to change is comparable to being poisoned. You don't see the devastating effects coming, but by the time you notice them it is too late. This books aims to remedy this "poison," hence the use of the word *antidote* in place of *anecdote*. The lesson in each chapter can be considered an antidote for change.

Why do changes need to happen?

Without change, there is no movement; without movement, there is no life. We seek change in life to adjust to our life situations. We all have life situations. Because of our life situations, we are forced to make decisions. A life without decisions would be a life without intelligence; but we all know that we were created intelligent beings.

Look at it this way. Every individual has been assigned a package. This package is your personal life situation.

When you are born, you open up that package and from that moment on, you will need to make adjustments in order to work with the elements of that package.

Many times change is the result of a decision. In order to function in society we must change. When we go from an infant to a toddler, we change. When we switch from a teen to a young adult, we change.

When we go from middle age to being elderly, we change!

At other times, change needs to happen automatically for the development of our well-being. When we traveling to high altitudes, our bodies change so that our cells still receive enough oxygen. Science shows us that we are constantly changing physiologically to stresses such as bacterial infections, air and water pollution, dietary imbalance, etc.

Therefore, a life without decisions is impossible. Our life is always moving, and decisions are always being made consciously and unconsciously through our bodies.

Why do we need reflections? Reflection is when one takes **time** to scan themselves and their surroundings. Reflections are our way of putting life itself under a microscope. Most importantly, reflections are a vehicle for change.

Once you understand why change needs to happen, and you have a great **attitude** in the midst of change, you will be ready to face challenges head on. It starts with taking **time** for yourself, to understand your surroundings and really push your progress forward. True and lasting change gives way to freedom. The keys to freedom must be found in the mind; they open the gates of the heart.

If you were to conduct an interview with yourself from 10 years ago, what would be your favorite article of clothing? What would be your favorite food? Car? Musician? Who would be the people you see on a day-to-day basis? What kind of hairstyle did you have?

The truth is, the person you are today is a stark contrast to who you were in the past. The culture around you has changed, your ideals have changed, and dare I say it ... a few morals have changed. To put it all in perspective, the only thing that remains the same is the aspect of change itself.

Change is one of the most dynamic elements of a human life, yet it's one that we understand the least. We are extraordinary beings living an ordinary life. Needless to say, the human race has a constant need for change realization.

This book focuses on change realization by using the following vehicles:

Storytelling- From the time we were in diapers to the time we are in a rocking chair, storytelling was, is, and always will be one of the most effective forms of communication.

Definition of key terms- The best way to construct a puzzle is to define the pieces you have to work with. Change is a puzzle, and it's not until we can identify its elements that we can truly get a grasp of it. Look for key terms highlighted in bold.

Action steps- It is great to read a good story and be inspired, but nothing comes to life until we actually do something with the information we have accumulated. Look out for these action steps at the end of each section.

Quotes- They can serve as brief reminders to keep

us focused on our goals. We put them on sticky notes on our desk, we put them on our walls in our bedroom, and we put them as our screen savers. Wherever we decide to put them, they will have a subconscious effect to the way we think, act, and feel. This book ends with quotes written by yours truly. Use them in your meetings, put them on your sticky notes, and memorize them so you can always have them with you.

Before we begin this journey, take a deep breath and repeat the following mantra:

Changes are necessary…

Changes are the vessel in which my life situation progresses …

Changes are necessary in order for me to achieve my purpose…

I am a vessel of change…

I am a vessel for my purpose…

Change is always working for my greater good…

There is no bad as it relates to change, only growth and expansion…

I am the embodiment of that expansion …

My lessons give me principles of success…

I use those successes as my testimony …

I am change …

Chapter 1

Change Realization

Chapter 1 - *Change Realization*

Change realization represents the life cycle of change.

Think about a newborn that is given a name at birth. Before the newborn was born, names were being contemplated. Parents name children after a favorite deceased relative, or they research a deep and meaningful name. Upon birth, the baby is given the name. Documents and the birth certificate are signed; the government is notified—but the name is not truly realized until the baby can consciously respond to it. After all, isn't this the purpose of having a name? So that one may respond and can be called by it?

Change works in the same way. Whether it's planned or unplanned, each change contains its own purpose. One can prepare or manage in the midst of change, but change is not complete until it is fully realized.

So here lies the question; how can change be realized?

There are two types of change. There is **anticipated change** (planned change) and then there is spontaneous change (unplanned change).

Both types of change require the use of the following three elements:

Education

  Attitude

  Technique

The acronym EAT.

Planned change requires these tools *before* the change occurs. Unplanned change will require these *after* the change has occurred. Ironically, even those who have weight loss goals must EAT to change. Change **education** means understanding the impact of the change that is about to take place. Identifying and exploring the change is the first step in change realization. In other words, we identify the pain points of this change, and decide if these pain points are worth the benefits of the change. A **Pain point** is any thing, person, or event that serves as a hindrance to change realization.

Education in the realm of change means understanding the benefits and risks. **Education** is a change shock absorber that lessens the potential of a gut-wrenching blow in the midst of life-altering change. Education is applied through research, visualization, and calculating the variables. A common tool for educating oneself on the impact of change is the use of the Start-Stop-Stay Method. When the change occurs, what will need to start happening? What needs to be eliminated (stop)? What can stay just how it is (stay)? By answering these questions, you can paint a clearer picture of what this change will look like.

Another common way to ensure proper education of a change is the use of B.R.A.I.N. What are the

BENEFITS of this change? What are the RISKS? What are the ASSUMPTIONS? What are the INTENTIONS? What happens if I do NOTHING?

Attitude in the midst of change involves a constant checking with yourself as it relates to your intentions and assumptions. In other words, what are your motives for each action that you take? Do you have pure intentions as it relates to an outcome of positive change?

Do your assumptions prohibit you from thinking clearly? Have those assumptions been proven, or are they meritless?

An **Attitude** is a settled way of thinking or feeling, sometimes about someone, but in this case about something. An attitude is almost always reflected in one's behavior. So when we talk about an attitude as it relates to change, we are talking about the settled thoughts and emotions that come with change. First, let's start with thoughts.

How do we perceive change? When a change works in our immediate favor, we think of the change as a "good" change. When the change looks to be a detriment to our immediate life situation, we think about it as a "bad" change.

The truth is, because of our conditioning, we are constantly trying to force elements in these categories of "good and bad." Change, however, does not operate that way. Change can always work for what we perceive as good. Our life situation can always benefit from change.

When it comes to thinking about change, we have to ask better questions. Instead of asking...Is this situation good or bad? It would be more beneficial to ask, how is this change going to intelligently pave a new way for something that is not yet here? No life situation is perfect. There are always adjustments that need to be made to the package.

This brings us to the second element: attitude. Feeling. When we think of a change as bad, then we feel bad about it. *Bad* meaning a harmony of unease in our mind and our emotions.

However, with the knowledge that change is universal, with the understanding that change is actually the expression of intelligence that is intelligently altering our life situation for good reason, we are more inclined to not take the abruptness of change as a personal attack. Our feelings will march in stride with our thoughts. Due to the years of conditioning and training to feel bad when we don't have immediate comfort, we have a lot of work to do when it comes to conditioning our bodies to be at ease in the midst of change; that is not easy.

Maintaining a healthy attitude in the midst of change is challenging. But adjusting with intelligence is a part of who we are as human beings. Dr Martin Luther King Jr. once said, "The ultimate measure of a man is not where he stands in moments of comfort and convenience, but where he stands at times of challenge and controversy."

Technique in the midst of change is the intentional actions taken before, during, and after a change has taken place. Actions without strategic intentions are just reactions. Action with a purpose is technique. Technique is the missing link between conquering difficult change and getting steamrolled by it. Great leaders lead with powerful technique. It is where the rubber meets the road, where the blueprint becomes the structure, and where the goals become accomplishments. True change realization is not just the completion of one changed life cycle; it's being prepared for the next transition. Doing "nothing" can be a technique within itself, not to be confused with ignoring issues or being lazy. In some cases, doing nothing until things become clearer is the wisest choice. In other cases, doing nothing can have catastrophic results.

For change to be realized, there are actions involved for the stakeholder. A stakeholder is someone who can affect or be affected by the actions of change. As a change stakeholder, it is important to become a student of change, to learn systematically how to make a positive and lasting affect.

Action Steps:

1. Choose one major change that you are currently facing.
2. Write down whether it was planned or unplanned.
3. Write down the Benefits and Risks of the change.
4. Create a Start-Stop-Stay (three columns on a piece of paper or white board) chart.
5. Write down what would happen if you did nothing.
6. If doing "nothing" has significant consequences, write down your strategic plan (action items just like these) that will need to be completed for this change to be realized.

Start	Stop	Stay

Example of a Start Stop Stay Chart

Chapter 2

Go to Class

Chapter 2 - *Go to Class*

Class is in session

In the eighth grade I had an English test that constituted 70% of my semester grade. The truth of the matter is, I was a lousy student, because I believed that certain subjects in school were "useless" and of no value to me. English was one of those subjects. I made a decision that, instead of studying and trying to learn the material, I was going to come up with a foolproof way to cheat.

I spent the next few days plotting how I would cheat on the final exam. Step one would be to write as many answers on the inside of my hand as possible. Step two was to write a few answers inside my desk on the day before the test. Step three was to pass a small piece of white lined paper back and forth between me and one of my coconspirators while the teacher was not paying attention.

On test day, everything was going smoothly. I had my answers well concealed, and I was ready to cheat.

Despite my natural gut feeling that something bad was going to come out of this, I proceeded anyway. In hindsight, all of the time I put aside to create ways to cheat, I could have been studying.

When the test was over, the teacher decided to read each student's score out loud. She had corrected the tests as soon as we passed them in. The only two high scores in the class were from Gloria and me. Gloria got an 85%, and I (not slick enough to throw in at least a few wrong answers) received 100%.

Our teacher then proceeded to give Gloria and me praise for getting such high scores. The sarcasm in her voice was cold-blooded. My heart started to beat fast as I began to realize that she was on to me. She then proceeded to ask Gloria and me to step in front of the room. My hands were so sweaty that the ink began to run from the answers I had written on my palm.

"Since you did such a good job, I would like you to demonstrate for the class how you solved these questions," posed the teacher in an intimidating, yet inquisitive tone. To my surprise, Gloria stepped up to the chalkboard and answered all the questions with ease. As it turned out, she had actually studied. When I went up, I froze.

"I forget," I said, feeling defeated and highly embarrassed. She told me to go back to my seat and to stay after class.

When class ended, I was told I would receive an F for the final exam, which, more than likely, meant I would get an F for the semester grade in that class. I remember feeling sick to my stomach for weeks. When the report card finally came, I opened it. I was fully ready to explain to my parents why I received an F. To my surprise, the grade was a B+ with a little comment next to it stating, "A pleasure to have in class."

Sometimes change can surprise us and work in our favor without any due diligence or any foresight. In fact, change can sometimes work in our favor even when we have made dreadful mistakes. The key is to not simply ignore your mistakes just because you can get away with them.

Take a moment and think about the following question honestly. Have you ever considered yourself to be a student? Not from a university, and not from a guru, but a student of life itself. If you can visualize life as your classroom, would you be a studious student? Every conversation, event, and incident is your lecture. Do you take notes from these events and learn from them? Opportunities to succeed are within your grasp, as every challenge is an open-book test.

Do you recognize your weakness and work on it? Or do you keep getting the same problems wrong over and over again? When given second chances, do you seize the moment? Or do you repeat the same foolish pattern?

Mistakes make for great professors, but the top-ranked teacher among them all is pain. It turns out that the teachers who have a personal touch are the most effective. **Pain** is that teacher. Seasons are semesters, and with each calendar year we can expect new lesson plans, pop quizzes, and tests that are more challenging, more advanced, and more significant than the year before.

How are your study habits? Do you review what is going on around you? Have you tried mapping out your goals, or do you go through the motions blindly, expecting better results?

Are you a good classmate? Do you make the members of your study group better or worse? When it's all said and done, when your name is called on graduation day, will it be followed by ear-popping cheers, or dreadful silence?

Nothing about this voyage of change and change education will be easy. Just like any final exam or all-encompassing test, as students, we must be ready to face the challenge.

Action Steps:

1. Name at least three pain points you are currently facing. It can be on a project, in a relationship, or

within yourself. Draw symbols to represent each pain.

2. Underneath each symbol, list the lessons that each pain point is teaching you.

3. Draw a big line underneath all of the above, then assign yourself a detailed homework assignment that will challenge you to face each pain point head on.

Chapter 3

Face the Challenge

Chapter 3 - *Face the Challenge*

Growing up, visiting Haiti taught me a great deal about perspective and the lack thereof. I can distinctly remember running around in the sweltering heat playing with the neighborhood children. When it was time to come home and bathe, I was stunned to find that there was no running water in the house. My mother directed me to the backyard, where I proceeded to fill a bucket with well water. It was then that it also occurred to me that the home we were staying at for the night had no electricity. All of the adults were sitting in the living room in pitch-black darkness when I returned that evening, having a normal conversation like nothing was wrong. The temp was in the low hundreds at the least. Mosquitos were all around, feasting on our flesh till we were covered from head to toe in bites. How could anyone live like this? I thought to myself. The truth is, to them this was normal. I was the outcast, the complainer, the privileged American that couldn't handle a few hot nights and a couple moments of being unplugged. Was I wrong for feeling uncomfortable? No.

Were they wrong in thinking that I was a spoiled brat? No.

What I know for sure is that it all comes down to perspective. After a few days, I was able to see that Haiti is actually a paradise in every sense of the word. The beautiful landscape began to captivate me. Being on the beach drinking cold coconut juice and living the simple life began to feel like second nature.

Whether it's a third world country or a wealthy nation, the fact of the matter is, we live on a beautiful planet filled with beautiful people. Contrary to what we see on the news every day there is bliss that can be obtained on earth; but it takes a change in attitude, habits, and perspectives to get there.

Once we get to a place where we know what change is, and we can have a healthy perspective towards change, then we are fully equipped to face the challenge.

The **challenge** is the element of the change situation that is going to test our abilities to bend. We can have all the knowledge and positive insight in the world, but still be tested. Just as the old saying goes "what we hope to do with ease we must first do with diligence." Challenge is our due diligence for getting change done.

Once we can accept change in our lives as necessary for our existence, then we also are giving ourselves permission to accept the endurance it takes for the challenge.

But similar to a boxer in a ring, it is not enough to simply brace ourselves for the challenge. No... we must face our challenger. We must meet the challenger head on, however many rounds it will take.

When a cyclist is attempting to finish a race and they come face to face with a steep hill, the only real option in order to finish that race is to pedal harder towards the hill.

The biker must use every part of their body to leverage themselves up the hill. The minute the cyclist stops pedaling, the finish line becomes further away. Why? The perspective has changed. Fear gives birth to a perspective of impossible.

It doesn't mean they won't reach the finish line; but there will be a major delay out of fear that it can't be accomplished. Ultimately the cyclist may miss the mark, and not reach their time goals.

The more we shy away from challenge, the longer it will take us to receive the results of our change. Delaying the inevitable may cause us to miss the mark, and skew our appropriate results.

We can't receive the results without the challenge. It is through proper perspective that we make it to our goals. We perform our due diligence to achieve our goals by facing the mountain and hauling ass.

Action Steps:

1. Identify at least one challenge that you are secretly petrified to face.

2. Close your eyes and imagine what life would be like with that challenge conquered. What does it look like? What does it feel like?

3. Identify your mountain.

4. Define what it means for you to pedal up that mountain.

5. Define what shift needs to happen in your perception in order for you to reach the top.

6. Draw a picture of your ideal situation using symbols, smiley faces, whatever you need to do to get the point across to yourself. Stick this picture in the middle of a notebook, book, or any folder you will use every day.

Chapter 4

Take a Time Out

Chapter 4 - Take a Time Out

One of the most complex elements that associates with change is **time**.

When change does not produce immediate results, it can give a false perception of being in a bad situation or circumstance.

For example: If you get laid off from a job, the immediate evidence looks bad. But when you get a job in a few months that is ten times more fulfilling, ten times more lucrative, and in alignment with your morals and standards, it doesn't look like such a bad change after all.

Hindsight is always 20/20.

You may find that many of the trials you have faced in your life turned out for the better in the end. Why is that? It is because the change accumulated time before it manifested into what we perceive as good.

Time is a vehicle that transports progress. With this in mind, in the midst of a change it would behoove us to take a time out.

What we do with a **time out** is simply retreat to a space where we are preparing ourselves for the progress that is about to take place.

A sports time out allows a coach to regroup with the players. This is usually during a major turning point in a game. When something is dramatically changing in the landscape of the game, the coach frantically pleads with the referee to call a time out. This is because the coach understands that during a critical change, there is a need to pull away from the situation and regroup.

Taking time out can mean many different things to many different people. The best way to look at it is that it's time for rest or recreation away from one's usual activities.

In the IT world, a common occurrence is systems that shut down or fail. This can be due to a multitude of reasons, but the main reasons for system failure is either because of too much "stress" on a system, or an unusual sequence of events that the system is not accustomed to handling. When one of these two situations happens, a system can shut down and it affects every person, place, or thing that is affiliated with it. It is referred to as an **unplanned downtime**.

Many of us live busy lives, and it may seem impossible to take a break; but when we don't take time off, our overworked mind, body, and spirit will take an unplanned downtime. This is where mental breakdowns, exhaustion, and depression come from. These breakdowns can cause us and the people around us to be negatively effected.

The principle is simple; either you take a **timeout** and regroup, or an **unplanned downtime** will shut it down for you.

Taking a time out also gives us a chance to be grateful for the things around us and the progress we made. William Arthur Ward once said, "Gratitude can transform common days into thanksgivings, turn routine jobs into joy, and change ordinary opportunities into blessings." Without taking a time out for gratitude, we can be setting ourselves up for some rotten days ahead.

By taking a time out, you are preparing the vehicle of progress for the road ahead. That vehicle is time.

Action Steps:

1. Identify a change you are going through that has yet to produce results.

2. Identify what you can do in this moment to prepare yourself for the results you desire. If the

changes correspond to your career, enter them on your calendar as a reminder. If the changes correspond to your personal development, write them on the bottom corner cf your bathroom mirror with a dry erase marker.

Chapter 5

Avoid Hell Days

Chapter 5 - *Avoid Hell Days*

A "living Hell" is a hellish experience that keeps playing out on and on as if it had a lifespan. Gospel artist Shirley Caesar once said, "I don't know about you, but I'm not going to live in hell and then die and go to hell!"

At some point we all go through what we call a day from hell. I can remember my first experience with management. I was leading a team for an implementation of medical software in Stockton, California. The team I was managing was under a great deal of stress. The schedule and timelines were tight, pressure was mounting, and as a result, tensions began to flare.

One day one of the managers from another team went to my direct reports and proceeded to chew them out. I stood by, mortified, as he picked each one apart. Finally snapping out of my trance, I got up from my seat and approached him. I am about 5' 11", and this man stood at about 5' 5". Looking up to me he began screaming at the top of his lungs for the whole office to hear. I guess the old saying is true that the small pot boils the quickest. I was enraged, but held my tongue. I couldn't help but notice this man was reckless. If I really had no control, I probably could have punted him across the room. The whole office stood by and watched in shock, most likely half-expecting me to do so.

I am sure he was stressed to the max, and the only way he thought he could deal with it was unloading on a group of helpless analysts. It was at that point that I realized I could either react as a victim and be as reckless as he was, or I could be empowered and make my way back to peace.

Later that day we were scheduled to be in the same manager meeting. The manager meetings were held in a tight boardroom with a long table and reclining chairs. I can remember giving myself a pep talk before walking in. I said to myself, "Michael, if you can control your thoughts, you can control your emotions, if you can control your emotions, you can make it through this meeting." I proceeded to walk in, and to no surprise, the manager was sitting at the end of the table in the king's chair, seething and giving me an intense, cold stare.

As the meeting went on, every time I went to speak I was immediately interrupted by this man. To set the scene it is important to note that this was a meeting that involved senior executives, directors, and managers.

"Let's talk about the third reason as to why…", I began to say.

" Yea, yea lets just talk about this third reason shall we!" The man interrupted.

" Excuse me do you have a problem?" I swiftly replied.

" Yea I have a problem, I have a problem with you!". He shouted while slamming his fist on the boardroom table.

Everyone was taken aback in pure shock and horror. One woman actually put her fingers to her lips and gasped, "Oh my". I took one long look at the man, crossed my legs, took a sip of my tea, and calmly stated: "Unfortunately that's not my problem.", I then concluded my train of thought with the group as if nothing had just happened. It goes without saying the man was swiftly fired immediately after the meeting. I was applauded for keeping my cool.

When a day turns sour its important to take time to gather your self and make an action plan. Becoming the victim does not leave room for real change. When it's a specific person giving you hell some times you have to let it go so you can grow.

Terrible mornings usually turn into terrible commutes to work, which turn into terrible meetings, which turn into terrible lunches and terrible afternoons. Terrible afternoons turn into terrible nights, summing up to a loaded day of ...you guessed it ... Terrible!

Why we have such days will forever be a mystery. There's hardly any pep talk that can get us out of a bad day, although many will try to "save" us from our bad day with words that anyone having a bad day hates to hear, such as: "it could be worse," "Look on the bright side," or the classic, "Someone out there has it worse than you." These words only make sense to the person who is speaking them. On the other end of that conversation you have someone who doesn't have the patience, inspiration, or temperament to entertain such theories. So, what can be done? What *should* be done? Is it really possible to turn such days around?

The truth is, when we have days like this we are the "victim," or at least we claim to be. With every new mishap that occurs in the day, we add it to our list of stories that we are building for ourselves. Our attention is solely on the things that are happening to us, and what will happen to us next. Unlike a hostage situation, we have the tools to create **contrary action**. In other words, we don't have to play a victim in our riveting bad-day drama movie. Instead of laying down, we can make a stand and use our energy towards something useful and productive. This scenario is much like the old story of the farmer and his dog.

The farmer and the dog are sitting on the front porch when a neighbor notices the old hound dog moaning and whining. Out of great concern of a serious injury the neighbor asks, "What's wrong with your dog? Is he hurt? Does he need to go to the vet? Is he dying?" "No," replies the farmer. "There's a nail poking out of the porch and he's laying on it."

"Well, why doesn't he just move?" the neighbor asks.

The farmer looks at the old dog and shrugs.

"I guess it doesn't hurt bad enough," says the farmer.

Action Steps:

1. When you have terrible days, what are the elements that bother you the most?

2. Identify ways that you can avoid being a victim in your own story.

3. Try going 24 hours without complaining once. journal about your experience.

Chapter 6

Welcome Pain

Chapter 6 - *Welcome Pain*

Can you remember a time in your life when you didn't see a light at the end of the tunnel? Can you remember a time when your circumstances where so grim that you believed that your life was cursed? Some of you reading this may be in this space right now. In fact, many people experience that; their life goes from one mess to the other, with very little relief in between.

There is no formula to eliminate hardship. There is no remedy to completely alleviate pain. Anyone who tells you otherwise is most likely feeding you propaganda. Pain is a necessary burden that serves a purpose in our lives. We run into problems when we can't come to a realization of what the purpose is or was. In addition, we dig up our past pain by referencing it in our memory, our current life situations, and our interactions with other people.

What if we made a commitment to ourselves to leave our past pain behind us? What if we let go of all the thoughts that did not make us strong? Letting go of hurtful thoughts is not ignoring problems. It is a conscious effort to remain grateful, humble, and inspired in the midst of it. It is being in the moment instead of wishing for momentum. It is a freedom from self-inflicted oppression.

How do we connect with a positive air in the midst of pain?

A study of drug abusers who quit found different rates of relapse among different addicts. Those who were externally motivated to quit, such as through a probation officer, etc., almost immediately resumed abuse. Those who were internally motivated, for personal health, etc., lasted about two years before relapsing. Those who replaced their addiction with new alternatives such as religion, developing a new work skill, etc., generally lasted eight years or more without relapsing, and the majority never used drugs again.

How were these people able to release the pain and

suffering of something as extreme as drug abuse, and break free?

Contrary action. Contrary action means you say, do, and think about what is good, what is loved, and what is peaceful. It means we shift our focus from pain to actively carrying out the things in life that matter the most. "I may have had a bad day, but what matters most is my kids, my health, my passions, my music, my art, my fishing, my golf, my softball, my novel, my bowling, my book club, my pen and paper, my yoga, my bike, my running trail, my weights, my Bible, my meditations, my whatever makes me feel good, is action to the contrary.

Have you ever watched a movie, and for the full 2-hour duration found yourself fully engaged with the characters and plot? For those two hours, the outside world becomes non-existent, and the only thing that is real at that moment are the characters in the film. It's no surprise that research shows that the local box office thrives during the heaviest recessions. A large part of that is because as humans, we desire an escape from our minds. This same escape can take place anytime, anywhere. Pain can only hold the mind hostage if we allow it.

Another element of contrary action is service. One of our essential needs as human beings is our ability to give. Goodwill towards others not only gives us a sense of fulfillment, but it also has healing powers that can mend the pains of both the giver and the recipient. As the old saying goes, "Live full, die empty!"

Someone very intimate with this concept is Chuck Feeney. Chuck is responsible for creating the "Duty

Free" empire. At one point he was considered one of the richest men on earth. Over his lifetime, Chuck has given away 7.5 billion dollars, almost all anonymously! He has been donating since the '80s, and it wasn't discovered until 1997. He has given 99 percent of his fortune to health, science, education, and civil rights causes around the world.

It is said that Chuck has about two million dollars left at the age of 82. He flies coach and wears a $15 Casio watch. When the media finally caught up with him to get his insight on why he was doing this, his reply was simple. Chuck stated he would rather use his resources during his lifetime than to let his money be frittered away after his death. Chuck claims that his vision is that the last check he writes in his lifetime will bounce.

Action Steps:

1. Identify the top pain points in your situation right now.

2. What contrary actions can you take today that can divert your energy and attention from the pain?

3. Record how each contrary action makes you feel.

Chapter 7

Bend not Break

Chapter 7 - *Bend not Break*

There comes a time in life when you are forced to get out of your pocket of comfort. This time can come often, or it can come few and far between.

The only thing that is certain is that this phase, this perfect storm, is very painful. It may feel like the ceiling of your life is slowly collapsing and there is no way out.

What happens when you can't get out? What happens when you are face to face with a collapsing ceiling and life has not granted you a way out?

In order to answer this question, we must first understand how we can take advantage of every and any situation. Even a falling ceiling.

Do you remember the hit show *MacGyver*? For those of you who are unfamiliar, MacGyver was a character that was able to create things from the simplest of household products. No matter what the situation was, no matter how severe, his creativity always got him out of a jam. This was a guy who used a chocolate bar to stop a sulfuric acid leak. He was also able to build a compass with some batteries, a cheese grater, a paperclip, and a cork. In one of his most dangerous moments, he rigged a vending machine to spit out cans to create a diversion from some armed criminals.

Why the MacGyver analogy? When we look beyond the confines of society, and look into the depths of our souls, we find this same creativity. We find an escape route that leads us to outer space. Are there astronauts in outer space concerned about a falling ceiling on earth?

Since we can't get into a spaceship to go to the moon, let's go to a higher place in our minds. With a perception shift, the agony can turn into triumph. The heartache can turn into love, and the pain can be turned into a lesson that will change your life.

This is why: When dark times come, we find new, innovative ways to bend, but we will never break.

You have two things that a bill collector, manager at

work, or an ex-significant other can never take away. You have your mind, and you have your heart.

As long as we have a belief, and the heart to persevere, we are never truly dead; never screwed, never broken. There is nothing in life more resilient and durable than the human spirit. In the face of terror and mass destruction, we as a people have proven time and time again that we can in fact band together and rise.

The problem we face with standing under a falling ceiling is not a lack of intelligence to find a way out... it's the fear that it is going to hurt. It is the fear of experiencing pain that keeps us from our creativity. It is this fear that makes us resistant to changes in our lives. It is the fear of pain that keeps us from truly understanding our power. Change creates creativity.

Creativity changes lives!

When we bend, we are figuratively taking a new form. We are creating a new shape for ourselves. No one teaches us how to do this. No one has the exact answer of what we are to do next. But we don't wait on an answer. If your roof is collapsing there is no time for self-hatred, no time for unconstructive criticism. There's only time for innovation.

Action Steps:

1. If your situation was in a TV show script and you needed to write a happy ending for your character, what would be the most innovative escape plan? Write this down, and be sure to identify all of the major characters.

2. What is standing in your way from innovating the way you did in your story? Write them down.

3. Write down action steps you can take to eliminate these challenges.

Chapter 8

Conscious Living

Chapter 8 - *Conscious Living*

Consciousness is the state of being awake and aware of one's surroundings. When we have a new understanding about something, our consciousness changes. We are now aware of new elements that we could have never seen before.

This happens often with change. Because of our new

consciousness, we see things and situations in a new way.

Have you ever been in the market for a new car?

You start to research for a new car.

When you have finally picked out the car, and have your intention set on buying it, something happens.

Now all of a sudden, everywhere you go, at every street corner stop light and parking space, you see the very car you have the intention of buying.

Is this a coincidence?

No.

You are now aware of the fact that this car is valuable to you. Now you can pick out the car in any environment effortlessly. Your new consciousness has made you on the lookout for this car.

Change can elevate our consciousness. We become aware of what is around us and the matters in our life in a whole new way.

In the same way that we embrace the change that is taking place, we must also embrace our newfound consciousness that comes with it. We must be aware.

Being aware of what?

Through all change, the highest priority is being aware of self. Be aware of yourself, your thoughts, your emotions, and how you proceed with your life.

Practicing this awareness on a daily basis is what we call conscious living.

We can turn what we have learned from change into the system of our beliefs. We can turn it into our chain of everyday reasoning. We can use the knowledge as a foundation of our success. The lessons we have learned through change are the best lessons that one can ever have. They are lessons learned through experience.

David Brinkley once said, "A successful man is one who can lay a firm foundation with the bricks others have thrown at him."

When it comes to consciously forgiving, let's consider

the stance that a newborn baby takes.

Since the day he was born, my baby hated to be on his back. Whenever it happened (diaper changes, changing clothes, etc.,) he would scream in agony and burst into tears. He would even take swings at my face, sometimes connecting a few jabs and a left hook. After the experience, he almost instantaneously reached up for my embrace.

With babies, forgiveness comes within a split-second. Even if I am the one inflicting discomfort on my newborn, I am still expected to be the comforter. There's no second-guessing, there's no questioning if I will harm again. It just happens instantly. There are no feelings of mistrust, there are no feelings of abandonment; only the bond of love and the constant need for that love. Call it naïve, call it being shortsighted, but there's something special about a baby's forgiveness.

Part of the reason they are so happy is that they don't hold on to anything. They don't have a filter that holds things for years, months, weeks, days, hours, or even a minute!

Are we aware of the space that resentment holds in our minds? What if we release those resentments and become consciously aware when we develop new ones. Being aware of animosity we have towards others is a giant step towards conscious living.

There is a difference between lessons learned in textbooks, and lessons learned from experience. I will never forget being in school, trying to memorize for a physics exam, and my professor told me don't memorize it... just know it.

When we learn lessons through experience, it becomes a natural part of our knowing. But to know something is to use it in practice. If I stop playing the piano for many years, it is possible for me to forget how to play some notes. But If I practice and play on a continual basis, I will be an accomplished musician till the day I die.

Our success means that we are reaching our goals. Our lessons are precious gems that we can use as a principle for achieving success in life.

A lesson learned is a lesson used!

Action Steps:

1. What are some elements you need to consciously let go in order to change?

2. Identify a recent lesson you have learned that you can implement immediately? Monitor your progress.

Chapter 9

Become a Great Leader

Chapter 9 - *Become a Great Leader*

An executive for a large multi-facility healthcare system was slated to retire. Part of his transition required choosing a successor. Within the company there were three candidates that potentially could fill the position. For about three months the executive contemplated who would be his successor. The first candidate was a sharp dresser with a mediocre work ethic, but was a slick talker. The second candidate was a seasoned employee who had been serving the health system in varying roles for over 25 years, but had a negative attitude and a false sense of entitlement. The third candidate had a modest resume, but a great attitude and work ethic. When it was time to make the decision, the executive turned heads when he selected the third candidate.

His reasoning?

- Fancy clothes can be bought with a salary increase.

- Technical jargon and lingo have their place, and ultimately can be learned over time.

- It's not enough to do enough to get by, even if you have been getting by for 25 years. Longevity doesn't always equal quality.

A great leader is made up of the intangibles, and exemplifies their best at all times. A great leader knows when to speak, and when to keep frustrations to him or herself. A great leader knows when to roll up their sleeves and dig in. Most importantly, a great leader knows how to maximize the moment and make the most out of every opportunity, no matter how much the odds are stacked up against them.

Mastering change is about maximizing the moment.

A boy lost his mother at the age of nine. His family was forced to become squatters. Moving from shelter to shelter, he had to hunt game at a young age in order to put food on his family's table. The father of this boy was illiterate, but this boy walked miles to find books to read. He later read the Emancipation Proclamation, and became one of the most influential presidents in this nation's history. His name was Abraham Lincoln. He grew up with next to nothing, but he maximized the moment and made history.

As a great leader, you have to be willing to work in the places people don't see. It doesn't necessarily mean you have to go around telling your story. Les Brown once said, "Don't go around telling people your story; 80% don't care, and 20% are glad it was you!" You can, however, use your story as leverage. You can look at your past as a way to maximize the moment. If you know what struggle is, then you should be able to recognize a window of opportunity that much more. Being a great leader of change means you maximize the moment, even in the most challenging of situations. The best way to master something is to become a leader. Leaders have no choice but to be evolved in their mastery. It is when we become the pioneers of change that we truly know what change really looks like.

Action Steps:

1. Write down the qualities that make you a great change leader.

2. Write down at least five ways that your leadership can evolve.

Chapter 10

What Change Looks Like

Chapter 10 – *What Change Looks Like*

We take change seriously because every part of our life is made up of change.

What separates good from great is the mastery of adapting to changing conditions.

Change realization is the full life cycle of change.

We must EAT to change; meaning we must *educate* ourselves, examine our *attitudes*, and use proper *technique.*

We do this by becoming a student of change, and dissecting all the elements that change has to offer.

After a thorough understanding, we roll up our sleeves and take action by facing our challenges head on, equipped with all of the information we have obtained by our analysis along the way.

Throughout this battle, we may need to step away and take time outs for perspective.

We may need to take time to acknowledge the accomplishments and progress made.

When change realization is on the brink, we may experience pain and "hell." This is, however, the greatest teacher, teaching us in ways we would never consider possible. It is important that when we are facing this pain to bend, but not break! All of this pain is just leading us to a place of consistency, which we refer to as conscious living. From this space we can be great leaders, ready to lead the charge. We always focus on the positive outcomes of change. When we are focused on the negative we will miss out on the progress we are truly making. It is the single most important process in life. With diligence we can all become agents of change.

Quotes

Quotes by Michael Maitre

"You can't create what you don't know and what you don't know will create you."

"A lesson learned is a lesson used."

"Challenge is our due diligence for getting change
done."

"When life hands you lemons...make organic Sprite!"

"Change creates creativity. Creativity changes lives!"

"Hard work always pays off. Even when there is no evidence of change. Change has already taken place within. Work hard, love hard, enjoy peace, live strong!"

"I will find new and innovative ways to bend, but will never break."

"You are a student of pain. Study the pain, and pass the test of life."

"If we allow our past to occupy our lives, we have no space for the future."

"In life we must be willing to give what we are asking for. Otherwise, we will never receive it."

"Too often we allow our dreams, visions, and aspirations to ride in the backseat, while our excuses ride shotgun."

"Life is a dance... you are either posted up against the wall, or you have a circle around you on the dance floor."

"Strive everyday to wake up and stay awake. Sleeping on the job will lay off your purpose."

"Your gift is the art; life is your canvas."

"You are not a victim of pain. You are a student!"

"When you are in agreement with greatness in your life, the greatness in your life will agree with you!"

"Keep going. Even when it hurts, success will heal in the end."

"There is no external measurement in this world that can ever calculate the depth of your infinite worth. You are worth every beautiful inch of space inside of you. True wealth resides on the inside."

"Many times, pain can be a great teacher. We must be willing to listen in order to hear the reason why pain exists. Why pain, and not something more pleasurable or comfortable? It is because pain is more effective, and is a great communicator of change."

"Peace is not the absence of war and chaos. It is its own dynamic force. Not to be confused with weakness. There is a powerful flow of good that is flowing everywhere."

"Be the first to change. It's contagious!"

"Help someone who can't return the favor...I dare you."

"Living is being alive while reaching potential. Existing is finding excuses while waiting to die."

"There is no failure, only training for the next best thing. Every form of defeat is a necessary consequence of engagement. Preparation is the pathway to victory."

"We are extraordinary beings living an ordinary life. "

"The keys to freedom must be found in the mind; they open the gates of the heart."

"Education is a change shock absorber that lessens the potential of a gut-wrenching blow in the midst of life-altering change."

"Time is a vehicle that transports progress."

Key Terms

Key Terms

Anticipated change- planned change.

Attitude- the settled thoughts and emotions that come with change.

Challenge- the element of a change situation that is going to test our abilities to bend. It is our due diligence for getting change done.

Contrary action- means you say, do, and think about what is good, what is loved, and what is peaceful. It means we shift our focus from pain to actively carrying out the things in life that matter the most.

E.A.T- stands for Education, Attitude, Technique; methodology needed for change realization.

Education- a change shock absorber that lessens the potential of a gut-wrenching blow in the midst of life-altering change.

Pain point- any thing, person, or event that serves as a hindrance to change realization.

Pain- teacher with a personal touch.

Spontaneous change- unplanned change.

Technique- the intentional actions taken before, during, and after a change has taken place.

Time- a vehicle that transports progress.

Timeout- retreating to a space. In this space we prepare for the progress that is about to take place.

Unplanned downtime- mental breakdowns, exhaustion, and depression.